# CONTENT

## COVER STORY | 6

**Charting Phenomenal Success of Inbox Income Academy**

Christian Bartsch, Publisher of BBT Magazine, introduces Gin Ng and Gavin Sim.

## PRODUCT STORY | 8

**Ahead of time - HUBLOT**

Christian Bartsch, Publisher of BBT Magazine, introduces:

The Hublot Big Bang Gold Ceramic watch.

&

The Innovative Watch Manufacturer Hublot.

# COLUMNS AND DEPARTMENTS

### HEALTH IN BUSINESS
**Discover your True Potential**
Sally Forrest — **10**

### BUSINESS STRATEGIES
**Achieve everything You want**
Mona Tenjo — **12**

### AUTOMOTIVE SUCCESS
**3 New Year's Resolutions for Car Dealerships**
Sam Komeha — **15**

### BUSINESS FITNESS
**10 steps to a Lean Business and increased Productivity**
Robb Evans — **18**

### FOUNDERS INTERVIEW
**For Entrepreneurs from Entrepreneurs**
Louis Kotze — **20**

### BUSINESS OPPORTUNITIES
**Are there Opportunities in Email Marketing?**
Gavin Sim — **24**

### INNOVATIVE COMMERCE
**AR increasingly impacts Customer Purchases**
Eren Ünlü — **11**

### DIGITAL TRANSFORMATION
**From a Centralized to a Decentralized System**
Yasemin Yazan — **14**

### PERCEIVED VALUE
**Deciphering your Investment Returns**
Kirstie Shapiro — **16**

### PROPERTY INVESTMENT
**5 Most Expensive Cities in Australasia**
John Stokoe — **19**

### MEDICAL STRATEGIES
**Why having Empathy is so important for Business**
Michelle Davis — **23**

---

## CONNECT WITH US

Read more Business Booster Today Magazine content at BusinessBoosterToday.com

Download the **Business Booster Today App** for iPhone or Android.

Like the **Business Booster Today Magazine on Facebook** for the latest news, photos, videos and exclusive online content.

Follow **@mybbtmagazine** on Twitter and keep informed on breaking news and busines trends.

View stories and photos on Instagram and get a backstage insight. Follow us at businessboostertoday

**Make connections** with fellow entrepreneurs and business people in our community at businessboostertoday.com

# FOUNDERS CORNER

## By Sue Baumgärtner-Bartsch & Christian Bartsch

**Business is about people. Building relationships, expanding into new markets and making your clients happy is a 365 day task to create success.**

2019 has begun and February is the start into the **Chinese New Year in Asia**. As we step into this new year of the pig, let us make sure that we set our intentions to be one of a good year, a year of prosperity and growth, and a year of building and monetizing relationships.

Why are relationships so important you may ask? **Asian culture** understands like no other that when you do business with others and enter into a business relationship, it is mostly about **trusting the other person that you do business with.** Collaborating with the right people and putting the right people in the right roles in your business matters in order to achieve the right results.

In no other continent has the importance of people in business played a major role.

Branding is important, sales is important, but understanding your customers and clients is key for your growth and that of your clients.

The Business Booster Today magazine has become the **#1 German Magazine for the Global Entrepreneur** with a global success team of 15+ amazing editors and ambassadors and **readers in 143 countries**. 2019 and the year of the pig has arrived and we are excited to boost people's lives and businesses to greater heights, profits and visibility. **As a media partner**, we work with and support keynote speakers, coaches, entrepreneurs and those who align with our vision of entrepreneurship, freedom of life and business.

Alone in the first months of the year, the magazine has grown by 3 people in our editorial team. Make sure that you **put the right people on your team** to success.

**Investing in the right people** who share **similar values** and join your vision and mission is what either makes or breaks your business. Build relationships with high value clients and potential business partners.

You need to work on your **sales, branding and systems**. Become branded by being in magazines and getting your story into the press. Nothing comes for free in this world. Watch the competition but even more so dominate your niche.

Each day, we make decisions; decisions that help us reach greater heights, leave us at our status quo, or make us die. Let's focus on growth and reaching greater heights. Growth to us means **collaborating with the right people** who share the same values, trust and vision. This means you create something bigger together.

2019 will be what we make it to be, and as entrepreneurs, lets empower many more people to live their dreams and fulfil their visions!

# EDITORIAL TEAM
## THE MOVERS AND SHAKERS
## THE DREAM TEAM

**Christian Bartsch**
Publisher & Editor in Chief

**Sue Baumgärtner-Bartsch**
VP & Interview Editor

**Orsi Beata Nagy**
Eastern Europe Editor

**Hazel Herrington**
Zimbabwe Editor

**John Stokoe**
Property Editor

**Silvija Popovic**
Croatia Editor

**Udo Bartsch**
Business Editor

**Jan Erik Horgen**
Norwegian Editor

**Melody Garcia**
USA Editor

**Greg JC Granier**
Fun & Speaking Editor

**Michael Knulst**
Netherlands Editor

**Eren Ünlü**
Technology Editor

**Aldrin-David Verburgt**
VIP Stylist

**Louis Kotze**
South Africa Editor

**Dalibor Kosic**
Real Estate Photographer

**Gábor Dobos**
VIP & Stage Photographer

---

## IMPRESS

**ISSN (Print Edition)**
2627-9223

**ISSN (Online Edition)**
2627-9231

**ISBN-13**
978-1-796598-67-4

**PUBLICATION DATE**
19.02.2019

**PUBLICATION SERIES INFO**
Asia Q1 / 2019 No. 1

**PUBLICATION REVISION ID**
2019-02303--1

**PUBLISHER & EDITOR IN CHIEF**
Christian Bartsch

**LEAD EDITOR & VP**
Sue Baumgaertner-Bartsch

**CONTRIBUTING EDITORS**
Udo Bartsch, Hazel Herrington, Jan Erik Horgen, Orsi Beata Nagy, Sylvija Popovic, John Stokoe, Eren Ünlü, Greg JC Granier

**CONTRIBUTING WRITERS**
Michelle Davis, Robb Evans, Billy Gajic, Raluca Gomeaja, Michael Knulst, Marina Kotze, Louis Kotze, Sam Komeha, Kati Israel, Jaine Lopez, Vikas Malkani, Robert Martin, Milos & Danijela Nakovski, Christine Nielsen, Nina Peutherer, Richard Peutherer, Gavin Sim, Nina Schmid, Kirstie Shapiro, Tomer Sapir Spitkowski, Cristina Stavinski, Mona Tenjo, Janine Van Throo, Yasemin Yazan, Brett Yeager, Erwin Wils, Sabine Zettl

**PHOTOGRAPHY, VIP STYLING & MAKEUP**
Gábor Dobos, Dalibor Kojic, Aldrin-David Verburgt

**PUBLISHED BY**
ACATO GmbH, 1st. Floor, Theresienhoehe 28, 80339 Munich, Germany

**ADVERTISING & SALES**
sales@businessboostertoday.com

Phone +49 89 54041070

www.businessboostertoday.com

**SUBSCRIPTIONS**
Booster club members: annual membership dues include €197 for a regular one-year subscription and €47 for an electronic member subscription. Non-members subscription rate are €97 for an electronic subscription. Change of address notices and subscriptions should be directed to BBT magazine.
Although BBT Magazine maybe quoted with proper attribution, no portion of this publication may be reproduced unless written permission has been obtained from the publisher.
The views expressed in this magazine are those of the authors and might not reflect the official policies of Publisher and its associated organisations.
The editors assume no responsibility for unsolicited manuscripts but will consider all submissions. Contributors' guidelines are available at businessboostertoday.com. Business Booster Today Magazine is a double-blind, peer-reviewed publication.

To order reprints, visit businessboostertoday.com or email info@businessboostertoday.com.

©2018 ACATO GmbH. "Business Booster Today", "Business Booster Today Magazine", "Booster Club", "Booster TV", "Crypto Booster Magazine", "BBT", the Magazine logo and related trademarks, names and logos are the property of ACATO GmbH, and are registered and/or used in Germany, the European Union and countries around the world.

All Content is protected intellectual property and may not reproduced without written consent of the publisher.

# CHARTING PHENOMENAL SUCCESS OF INBOX INCOME ACADEMY

## Gavin Sim & Gin Ng

### By Christian Bartsch (Publisher/Germany)

Taking risks to invest in the vision and make a mission reality is what characterises true entrepreneurs. As I would find out, the founders of Inbox Income Academy, Gin Ng and Gavin Sim, **epitomise the spirit of taking risks and making innovation**.

### The Founders

Let us take a look at Gin Ng. In 2012, having no backup plans whatsoever, he invested his entire savings into his online business and worked part-time on it for three years. By 2015, Gin succeeded in gaining financial freedom and now passively earns 15,000 - 20,000 USD per month. He proved himself as an action taker and is a hard worker who executes plans fast and has the flexibility to adjust along the way. His talents include being not only very tech-savvy but also being able to explain complicated concepts in straightforward terms.

Now, let us turn our attention to Gavin Sim. Gavin is a former Captain in the Republic of Singapore Navy and rose to become the second-in-command of a warship. Responsibility and leadership are ingrained in this exceptional entrepreneur, and you know it the moment you speak to him.

Entrepreneurship manifests in his early stage, and he started selling Disney birthday cards (printed from his computer at home!) when he was 8. A visionary who values integrity and quick implementation of ideas, Gavin started Internet

Marketing in 2012 on by selling advertisements when he read that he could make money online by doing so. Apart from his military and internet career, his business experience also includes having been a Director of Business Solutions for an international magazine.

### The Beginnings of an Empire

After having met at an Internet Marketing event, Gin and Gavin found that their vision was aligned to help more people achieve financial freedom through email marketing. With that in mind, they founded Inbox Income Academy (IIA) on 1 Jan 2018.

Today, Gavin and Gin are much **sought-after International Speakers and Coaches**. Their programs and classes were innovative and very well-received. Success stories of their clients and graduates are coming out on such a regular basis that they caught my eye when I meet them in the United States which eventually lead to this interview and feature.

When Inbox Income Academy first started, they were solely focused on making Internet Marketing courses better. "We saw that many courses were theory-based and students had no idea what to do after the course. That is why we created our Fast Start program where our students have a working and revenue generating business in two days," said Gin enthusiastically. "**Essentially, we have created an action program where the students will learn, plan, create, and launch their business in two days. It is intense,** " added Gavin.

Inbox Income Academy's core

values include Integrity, Honesty, and Fun. When asked why, Gavin said, "I believe that Integrity and Honesty are very important because, in our industry, reputation matters and news spread very quickly. Perhaps it is also due to my military background that I want our business to be upright and always to do the right thing. No funny business." At this juncture, Gin quickly added that "Fun" was his idea because Gavin is way too serious at times and "Fun" is a way to balance their characters in the company and he also wanted to portray that **the internet business is delightful.**

### Innovation at the Forefront

While the coaching front was growing, Gin and Gavin were already innovating to help their students and clients to get ahead. While the Fast Start Program coaches students to generate an additional stream of income online through email marketing, the duo knew that they had to innovate to move ahead of the game by helping the clients to manage and maximise the potential of their business.

"That is where the Assets Under Management Program, or AUM, comes in," said Gavin. "Fast Start helps to get an individual started, while AUM gathers the strength of everyone to explode onto the scene," explained Gin.

Exploded they have. As I was sitting with these gentlemen, they showed me how within two months, they gathered more than 270,000 USD and were competing with veterans of their industry who had more than ten years of experience. In fact, in recent competitions, they were ranked top. "We opened doors that were previously shut to individuals. **We want every single one of our clients and students to succeed,**" both said together.

Exploring new frontiers are the duo's expertise. It has helped them step up their game. For example, they took ad-hoc unplanned and unprofessional advertising on Facebook to well designed, scheduled and monitored advertising campaigns. **That drove their cost per lead massively down and helped them create a new source for leads where the traditional email marketers depended on buying from other list holders.**

As of writing, Inbox Income Academy has helped countless people start their business online and make a living. I was just blown away by the number of testimonials that the Academy have gotten.

However, **the duo is not resting on their laurels and are already plotting their next industry-disrupting move**. "The next move is to help businesses, clients, and students to get their talents and knowledge online where it can be sold. Currently, they have to do it all, but we have a program where Inbox Income Academy can do it for them," teased Gavin. "It is currently in the testing phases, and the results are very encouraging, "said Gin.

Both founders are forward-thinking entrepreneurs who are consistently at least eight steps ahead of their market. Within a short period, they went from conducting paid courses and seminars to managing clients'

assets, and now creating bestselling products. Who knows what else they can come up with?

### Giving Back to the Community

Inbox Income Academy knew that they came from the ashes and had very humble beginnings. As such, giving back is very important to the founders. Confident in the value they deliver, they offer free weekly online webinars on Facebook which are watched by beginners and industry experts alike. Consequently, many followers became passionate fans of their coaching and educational content. **The superb support from the team and founders ensures that their clients reach their goals and their client base grows week by week.**

"Another thing we realised is that support is often lacking in this industry. That is why we offer our clients and students the best support that they could possibly have - direct access to us," said Gin. "We have no expectations when we give back. However, sometimes, when you give more, you gain more in return," added Gavin.

### The #1 Email and Affiliate Marketing Academy in the World

The uniqueness of Inbox Income Academy is the quality of coaching and the business expertise of the duo. Their unique approach of leveraging the opportunities of making money with affiliate marketing and combining it with a proactive strategy that differentiates them from the so often seen passive marketing approach.

The programs, in the clients' and my opinions, are very holistic and individualised. Gin and Gavin understood that each client is different and that their needs are different, much like the risk appetite of each client. They do not force everyone to take a single approach but instead, help each craft their unique success path. This approach has a well-documented system that **ensures the success and profitability of each client.**

People often underestimate the work schedule of email and affiliate marketing entrepreneurs. These hard-working people have to adapt their work time to the times when their community database is receptive for engagement. Working from Asia, the duo often pulls long nights to guide their clients based in Europe or the Americas. Therefore, it is also not exaggerated to say that Inbox Income Academy's contributions to their community are way beyond Singapore's borders.

Inbox Income Academy's approach to business, life, and coaching combined with excellent quality and commitment impressed me deeply. I have spoken or have interacted with many other academies that do similar courses, but **Inbox Income Academy is a few classes above any others**. To achieve the kind of success within this short period is truly incredible and amazing.

Business Booster Today is proud to name Inbox Income Academy as the **World's #1 Email and Affiliate Marketing Academy.**

# AHEAD OF TIME

## Hublot's - BIG BANG UNICO KING GOLD CERAMIC

### By Christian Bartsch (Publisher / Germany)

### Entrepreneurs trust Hublot

In life there are a few very valuable elements that will not last forever. This is where time is a significant influencer of a person's success. If you do not make good use of your time, you lose business opportunities, deals and unforgettable experiences. That is why successful entrepreneurs take care of this valuable resource by trusting their particular brand of watches.

There exists a definite difference between high precision designed watches and the imprecise cheaply made watches. The price tag gives a relative impression of the **time and effort** that goes into the making of a high quality watch. In the watch making industry there exists a wide range of quality levels.

When you look at the engineering skills that go into a Hublot watch then you see this is not something you can mass produce at low pricing. A valuable long lasting product requires technical expertise but also a feeling for beauty.

### Hublot stands out

That is where Hublot displays a focused but stylish variety of designs. When you invest **4 years** into developing the technology and design for the Unico movement then you must definitely admire their wonderful results.

As previously remarked, this is not a mass production product. It has 330 individually hand assembled components. That makes up the unique and distinguished movement of this watch. Although the complexity of this product is so massive, the engineers were already 8 steps ahead in their thoughts. They were able to allow the system to be even **upgraded to include** additional complications and modules.

Who else is able to add the Flyback Chronograph, GMT or the Bi-Retrograde Chronograph? That is what gives Hublot the competitive advantage in its own market niche.

### Hublot is Sports and Luxury

Entrepreneur needs to keep fit. A passion for sports requires a watch that is reliable and can take on the dynamic life of its owner. When you look back in time, you must recognize that when **Carlo Crocco** founded Hublot in **1980** he wanted to combine luxury and sports.

### Why Crocco founded Hublot

He was a passionate sailor and unsatisfied with the metal bracelets and leather straps solely available at the time. This kind of material had a great disadvantage when in contact with water. That is when **he chose rubber** as the better partner of a watch that will accompany its owner – "*whatever the weather and the sport*."

Being **ahead of the industry** eventually made Hublot an industry disrupter. Rubber became the product other watch manufacturers adopted after they had to accept that **Crocco had made the best decision** for this type of application.

Even then knowing the tear and wear that a sports watch will be submitted by its owner, Hublot makes use of Ceramic to substantially remove the risk of its products accumulating signs of wear. Ceramic is considered to be a **scratch proof material** naturally protected against signs of aging.

The manufacturer's research and development department is working ahead of time to astonish its clients with new products. These can have a bright red or yellow ceramic touch.

When it comes to the **Big Bang Unico Gold Ceramic** you need to step back and admire the composition:

The casing is a polished and satin-finished **18K King gold** case. The bezel is a stain-finished black ceramic anodized black Aluminum lower bezel with **6 H-shaped titanium** screws. The dial is a magnificent mat black dial and gold-plated upper layer.

The **satin-finished indexes** include a white luminescent. Furthermore, the satin-finished and micro-blasted **gold-plated hands** come with a white luminescent, too. As highlighted, rubber is the material used for the black structured lined straps.

If you are new to high quality watches, then you know how annoying it is to have to get a new battery every few months.

With a Hublot you are better off. This watch comes with a **self-winding** chronograph system. As you move during the day, the watch makes use of the owner's lifestyle to rewind itself. Hence, you also avoid forgetting to wind up your watch manually. Even if you do not move, the watch has a **power reserve of 72 hours**.

Hublot's success shows in its contribution to the community. By being a luxury and innovative brand, the business has been expanding. The plant built in Nyon **doubled its surface area within 6 years** of opening that plant in 2009.

The competitive advantage of Hublot is based on the combination of traditional mechanical movements using *principles dating back 300 years* while using the latest technology, materials and processes.

That is why it makes Hublot the prefered watch for sports loving entrepreneurs, artists and professional athletes. Famous Football managers like *Jose Mourinho*, Football icons like **Diego Maradona**, the golfer *Dustin Johnson* & *Patrick Reed* and Boxer *Floyd Mayweather* are passionate Hublot watch owners.

### Where gold comes gold unites

Olympic gold medalist Usain Bolt won 8 gold medals and 11 world championchip titles. Hublot watches acompany him on his path to

success and contribute to good causes that help preserve traditional cultures.

Hublot watches are also a part of successful women. Tennis star Simona Halep and Karolina Pliskova love the watches for their beauty and sportiveness. The **supermodel Bar Rafaeli** is a huge fan of Hublot and the first female face to represent the brand.

Being at the top of the game is not easy. The **Australian** cricket team Captain *Michael Clarke* and the explosive **Indian** cricketer batsman *Rohit Sharma* are great brand ambassadors for Hublot.

If you are not into sports but love music then you will love the harmony of a Hublot Big Bang Unico Gold Ceramic clock system. Even the artists and musicians of *Depeche Mode* are part of Hublots activities. That is where business, craftmanship and music come together to help people gain access to clean and safe drinking water to people in developing countries.

### Craftmanship and innovation

Hublot is the ultimate love for craftmanship combined with innovative thinking. Hence, an entrepreneur who believes in the sport of business will also believe in the business of sport.

When in need of sportive precision, you will find a Hublot watch all around the world in their specialized boutiques. To find the authorized dealers just visit the manufacturers website for a directory:

www.hublot.com

# DISCOVER YOUR TRUE POTENTIAL, YOUR BUSINESS STYLE AND SUCCESS WILL BE YOURS

### By Sally Forrest (Singapore)

Have you ever wondered why some years are more successful than others? You are in the flow of life and opportunities are endless? Other years are the absolute opposite, you feel like you are "wading through treacle" and nothing is working? Ever wondered why some partnerships work out and others turn into a disaster? Ever wondered why suddenly legal issues arise and people stab you in the back?

The answers are found in the ancient **Chinese Metaphysics Wisdom** and after 15 years of study I have unlocked the secrets and found the manual or the blueprint to life. It's almost like finding the "jigsaw puzzle of life" and being able to piece it together for everyone as an individual. Amazingly everyone's jigsaw looks different and once the components and the overall image is explained and seen, then life becomes smooth sailing. Imagine being able to clearly see your innate gifts, to bring these out and to make the most of the maximum success periods of your life. By forecasting patterns, applying wisdom and turning data into intelligence, I have a systematic way of predicting the future trends for clients and business. In positive periods, it is all systems go and my advice is to "squeeze out the juice" in all aspects of life. However, life is not all smooth sailing and by identifying periods of challenge, my clients are able to be forewarned and take appropriate measures.

So, what is the secret code?

It's simple, you were born with the code. It's like your personal barcode. The moment you are **born there exists an energy.** The ancient Chinese 10,000-year calendar converts your exact time of birth into **a series of 8 characters**. These characters can have a **Yin and a Yang component** and belong to one of 5 elements namely **Metal, Water, Wood, Fire and Earth**. The combination is unique to you, and has to be carefully unlocked by an expert who takes into consideration many other important factors like your gender, whether you are a twin etc. The unique combination is then affected by **annual energies**, **luck pillars** and monthly effects, so it is not static, its constantly in motion and each layer needs analyzing individually and as a whole.

The analysis is not based on filling out a "general questionnaire" online or "reading one of 12 horoscopes", which appears to be the trend in today's society. This approach literally says you fit into one of 12 "categories" which is too general and limiting. I find this approach dangerous as you are making decisions for your life based on basic guidance about the animal year of birth, which is only one of the 8 elements. The year of birth is the least important aspect, it is your **day of birth and its interactions with the 8 elements that holds the secrets.** So, remember garbage in, garbage out and be cautious! The whole world is not simply categorized into one of 12 broad brush categories, if only life was that simple.

Individual Consultations

Those who have experienced my bespoke consultation know the **depths and accuracy** of the readings and **strategically plan ahead** to maximize every opportunity. Some charts have all 5 elements in them, which is often interpreted as balanced with the ability to utilize all 5 skill sets. However, a balanced chart can also show lack of drive and ambition with no strong desire to lead the race or stand out. Other charts are extreme, only one or two elements in the whole chart. These are the special ones, born with a clear gift and a deep driving passion and desire to follow their dreams no matter what. One element leads the way and once this one element is understood and followed then nothing will stand in the way of success. However, in **years when this element is clashed**, that's when you need to **be ready for fireworks and drama. My mantra to all my clients is "Don't Do Drama"** and so we strategize and plan ahead to smooth the waters. The Yin and Yang components need to be considered – **when do you act and lead from the front and when do you plan and strategize** and not raise your head above the parapet. Sometimes working in silence is the solution.

Can you share some examples?

One of my clients, worth over $200 million, consults each year to see how the charts of senior managers in each of his businesses is affected by the year's elements. I then guide with wisdom on who should be the front for each business, who is likely to have emotional / betrayal issues and who will be the star of the year and so receive the most demanding roles. Individual clients consult to understand their own strengths and to see how their interpersonal relationships can be improved within the family / business unit. CEO's call me to get immediate answers to issues as they arise thus aiding their decision making. Parents consult me to fully understand their child's skill sets and strategies for success and happiness in life. I have been consulting for over 10 years and have a loyal following of clients since their first consultation as the predictions and strategies always work out. I work in strictest confidence and our discussions are discrete and focused. I am able to combine the wisdom with my 18 years of business experience and so issues such as partnerships, JV, Licensing, takeover, M&A, recruitment, restructuring can also be included.

What about 2019? What is in store?

**2019 is the year of the Earth Pig**. It starts on the **first day of Spring in the Chinese Calendar**, 4th Feb. This means the **elements of Earth and Water dominate** the year and these elements add to and influence your own chart in different ways. Earth and Water are "clash elements "as water is prevented from flowing easily by the earth. This has a few meanings, and the overall chart has to be analyzed for a complete reading. Allow me to share the themes of the year.

1) Turbulence and Change will dominate the year. There will be a stop/start effect as progress made is then stopped.

2) Leadership battles and super power competition is the theme in governments and business. On the surface all may appear well and similarities are there, however underneath it is not all plain sailing, and stubbornness will delay solutions.

3) Muddy waters mean lack of clarity so allow time for the mud to settle before deciding on new deals and partnerships.

4) The outside appearance of 2019 is Yin, one of a more passive year, however within the remaining elements of the year it's totally Yang. This implies behind the scene activity and aggression. What you see in 2019 is not what you get.

The elements of the 2019 Pig Year need to be analyzed taking into consideration your personal chart as **there are treasures to be found** in the muddy waters of life.

# AUGMENTED REALITY ("AR") INCREASINGLY IMPACTS CUSTOMER PURCHASES

## By Eren Ünlü (Turkey)

As indicated by the exploration in the third quarter of 2015 (Mobile Path to Purchase, 2015) report in today, up to 60 percent of mobile device users exclusively make their purchase decision online.

According to Forbes, 74 percent of people use their mobile phone to help them while shopping, with 79 percent making a purchase as a result. (ImpigeMobileStrategy.com, 2015). The mobile phone has become a convenient shopping destination for most of the online population. It can be said that mobile shoppers tend to engage in more casual browsing behavior. Augmented Reality (AR) is the technology to create a "next generation, reality-based interface". AR supplements the real world with virtual objects that appear to coexist in the same space as the real world. AR has been used with developing technologies on mobile devices such as mobile phones, tablets etc. Besides this, mobile users make their purchase decisions on mobile ecosystem. New technologies such as QR code, mobile social media, mobile AR, etc. are attracted by the consumers. Thus, they tend to try, use and transform their behavior toward mobile purchase.

**Mobile AR** is the **latest technology** which has been used in a variety of **marketing campaigns as a remarkable medium** for consumers to **interact with a brand**.

On the other side, traditional e-commerce systems often cannot provide enough direct information or product interaction for consumers. AR methods and applications have been improved significantly over recent years; there has been little research related to usage of AR for magnifying e-commerce. The statement explained above is a deficiency about mobile purchasing.

### Augmented Reality

Augmented Reality (AR) can be thought of as the "middle ground" between virtual environment and telepresence. According to AR system:

· Combines real and virtual objects in a real environment;

· Registers (aligns) real and virtual objects with each other;

· Runs interactively, in three dimensions, and in real time.

Augmented Reality (AR), an emerging Human-Computer Interaction technology, which aims to mix or overlap computer-generated 2D or 3D virtual objects and other feedback with real world scenes, shows great potential for enhancing e-commerce systems. The new approach gives customers a chance to "try" a product at home or in another usage environment. Augmented reality simulates enough of a "**direct experience**" with a product in order to make an impact on the user. There have been a few real-world examples of augmented reality being used to enhance mobile shopping processes. There are AR platform companies such as Layar, Wikitude, Vuforia which supply mobile AR project design tools for marketers. Since the beginning of 2010's some mobile AR commerce projects were designed with these tools such as AR application for Publishers Weekly magazine, Mr. Porter the online retailer, Ikea the furniture retailer, Audi etc.

All **mobile AR applications** intent to **change consumers' behavior** toward their product or service. Overall results of the study will show that the AR mobile commerce system can **help customers make better purchasing decisions**.

### Image Interactivity Technology (IIT)

Interactivity is regarded as an important feature for e-commerce ecosystems to attract consumers' intention. The significance of interactivity is increasing in mobile commerce environment. Image Interactivity Technology is used to simulate actual experiences with the product or environment. Such as, virtual reality technologies fully involve online consumers inside a digital environment. According to online retailers, they make efforts to treat their visitors/customers well in terms of incorporating advanced image interactivity technology (IIT) to provide 3D virtual experiences and facilitate viewers to simulate the actual experience with the product or environment. And it is found that 3D presentations of products outplayed 2D presentations to increase perception of indirect (virtual) product experience online. IIT allows customers to select images of products and body attributes meeting the customer's individual specifications, then see what the products would look like. In accordance with former studies about IIT factors' effects Augmented Reality technology allows consumers to **zoom in on product features, rotate and view the product from different angles** and view the product in various colors on a virtual model created to imitate consumers' appearance. With image interactivity technology (IIT), product's design features, background, context, viewing angle or distance **can be changed by the user** and the product's features on the digital environment can be visually experienced, product information through visual indications can be strengthened.

### Telepresence

Telepresence is described as the experience produced by a computer-mediated environment, such as **trying on store products** produced by virtual modeling technology. To describe the perception of the realism of a computer-mediated experience, telepresence is defined as **a sense of presence in a mediated environment.**

In order to the explain telepresence, a sense of presence in a remote environment, is used to examine the process by which media characteristics influence consumer responses. Besides, telepresence is affected by level of image interactivity technology. The concept of telepresence can thus be applied to consumers when they interact with products presented in 3D. More specifically, telepresence requires that how closely the quality and quantity of simulated sensory information about the product and the simulated ability to interact with the product approximate the sensory information from interaction with the product in the real world. The two major factors of telepresence are **interactivity and vividness**. Interactivity refers to consumer interaction with products; while vividness represents the representation richness of product demonstrations. It was found that there is a positive impact of visual product experience or telepresence on online consumer responses and it was found that telepresence affected consumer responses indirectly by **simplifying product knowledge**.

### Purchase Intent

Purchase intentions were examined to explain behavioral responses. AR produces a higher level of product knowledge caused by virtual experience conditions and unveil a significantly positive effect on attitude and purchase intent.

Therefore, the emergence of purchase intention caused by mobile marketing activities is on account of product knowledge and attitude.

# ACHIEVE EVERYTHING YOU WANT

## By Mona Tenjo (Germany)

Would you also like to achieve more in your life? Reach more goals? Get more results? Have more impact?

As entrepreneurs, we always look for ways to improve ourselves.

**Secrets to getting anything you want**

In the past few years, many people asked me how I get so much done. In the beginning, I was surprised because I was not even aware that I am finishing so much more than others. However, looking at the facts, they were right. So, I analyzed what I do differently than many people around me – my "secrets to getting anything you want":

1) **Focus:** Focus on a maximum of three projects at the same time. These are your most important areas that you want to move ahead.

2) **Priority:** Whenever you do something, pick a clear priority! What do you need to do that is more important than anything else? Focus your energy to what is most important, otherwise, you get nothing done.

3) **No Excuses – just do it:** This one is essential. We all make bold commitments when we are in the mood to change something. However, when it is time to implement them, your brain is great at talking you out of it again. Thus, do not allow your brain to take control over you. When you said, you would do something, just do it!

4) **Plan time for what is important to you:** If you want to achieve a goal, you need to allocate time to it. This is not only true for business goals but for any goal. Health or relationships don't maintain themselves. You need to allocate time to it. Things that don't make it on your agenda are not important to you. They will never be done if they are not on your schedule! When they are on your schedule – just do it!

5) **Track your progress:** All planning and focus doesn't help if you don't track where you are heading to. Reaching a long-term target takes time and there are many possibilities to slip off track. Therefore, you always have to keep an eye on your progress, track your numbers, and measure your results. This way, you can intervene if something unplanned happens.

6) **Don't quit:** I mean this: Don't quit! EVER! Quitting is a bad habit that you have to avoid at all times! Yes, sometimes it will be tough and yes, you will not make a big step forward every day. However, stick with it! Competitors outperform most entrepreneurs only because they didn't quit! Hang in there and continue making small steps forward. They add up over time!

7) **Accountability:** Always get somebody to hold you accountable. As said above, your brain is great at talking you out of decisions! If you have somebody external to hold you accountable on your targets, it keeps you on track. Pick somebody who will not accept your excuses! It doesn't help you if somebody has pity with you and accepts all your apologies!

8) **Distraction Defense System:** You must create a system that helps you defending yourself from any distractions. Identify what distracts you the most during the day, and then start implementing mechanisms to prevent these interruptions. This will increase your productivity incredibly!

**What else do you need to know?**

Now that you have my personal secrets to getting everything you want, I have two final points that really elevate your results:

1) Set goals the right way: If your goals are unrealistic, not measurable, not specific enough, not attractive for you or missing a clear timeline, then you won't be successful. Such type of goals will only frustrate you. Thus, set yourself goals that you want to achieve, that you can measure, that are very specific, that are realistic and of course that have a fixed timeline.

2) To reach your goals, create yourself an action plan. Take your big goal and break it down into smaller targets, so-called milestones. Little chunks that you need to achieve in order to achieve your big goal. Also, consider in which sequence you need to implement these steps. Then you simply execute your action plan. Don't look at your huge, impressive overall goal every day! This might demotivate you! Track against your action plan of the current week! Since you dissected your big goal into milestones, you focus on and measure against these milestones.

When you take a look after a few month, you will be surprised how far you've come already!

# DIGITAL TRANSFORMATION

*From a centralized to a decentralized System Architecture*

## By Yasemin Yazan (Germany)

### 1. What is Blockchain-Technology?

The term is mostly associated with cryptocurrencies. You need to look at the underlying technology, the opportunities which come up with this technology and what exactly this means for the market of the future – the blockchain technology.

First, let me explain in simple terms what that is:

While centralized networks are used today to transmit information, data, and transactions, Blockchain technology transmits them through a network of independent computers from people like you and me scattered around the world – a so-called decentralized network.

### 2. How does it work?

To illustrate how the system works, let's take a financial transaction as an example:

If you want to transfer money today, a centralized network will be used where a trusted third party, e.g. a bank, is needed. This third party must first identify and verify the participants. Only then will the transaction be executed and stored in an in-house cash book for traceability. That costs time and money.

The principle of blockchain technology must be presented in several steps to make it plausible:

Let's assume that several people want to transfer money using blockchain. In contrast to the in-house cash book an open cash book is used, which everyone can see. This means that every transaction that is made is recorded in this cash book. Thus, if A transfers money to B, it is registered there, just as when person B transfers money to person C, etc. This concept of open cash book is thus a chain of transactions that can be viewed by each participant in the network. Based on the knowledge from the open cash book, it is then possible to allow or reject transactions. So, if someone wants to transfer a sum of money that he doesn't have, the other participants in the network would know, reject the transaction and not save it in the cash book.

But an open cash book alone is not enough, otherwise we would have a centralized network that would be used again. Therefore, there is not only a single open cash book, but each participant of the network can run his own cash book. This creates a decentralized network, which ultimately makes the central open cash book superfluous and unnecessary.

But somehow it has to be ensured that all decentralized cash books are in sync. And this is ensured by the use of so-called miners. Miners are a type of exam unit that compete with other miners. They each have two tasks: First, the miner checks, based on their cash book entries, whether the transaction is valid by looking to see if the person wishing to make a transfer also has the money. Second, he must find a key code to link the unvalidated transaction with his cash book. To find the right key randomly, a computing power is required. Figuratively, you could say that the miner is trying until one of the keys fits.

The miner, who first finds the right key, enters it with the transaction in his own cash book and is rewarded with a small amount. He also provides the key to the network. Now all other miners also enter this transaction in their cash books, because it makes no sense for them to continue to search for a key, because they wouldn't get paid for it. Instead, they would rather search again for the next transaction, which has not yet been assigned a key, which is why there is again the possibility that they can earn money from it. This principle therefore ensures that the cash books are all synchronized and the network remains running.

In summary, there are three key aspects that make up the blockchain technology:

- There is a public cash book where transactions are linked as a chain,
- this cash book is not centrally held and controlled by one authority, but distributed decentrally across the network,
- the miners organize and secure the transaction in the cash book and receive a small amount of money for this.

### 3. What does it mean?

Thus, Blockchain-Technology offers some unbeatable advantages:

- Decentralization and cryptical procedures ensure a high level of security.
- This infrastructure provides the ability to send financial assets and sensitive data without being reliant on a middleman.
- The transactions stored in the blockchain cannot easily be changed.
- The system is transparent, as all transactions and data can be tracked.

### 4. Relevance to the question of "How to Dominate your Market"

If you understand the principle of blockchain, then it quickly becomes clear that this technology offers incredible opportunities for the future, as its capabilities are almost limitless. So it does not matter if and if so which cryptocurrency prevails. In contrast, the technology used in the background is relevant. This technology or one in more advanced form will prevail. So it makes sense to look at it today and think about which products and business ideas, regardless of the industry, can be developed. With a corresponding idea and strategy, this technology, especially in combination with other technological advances such as artificial intelligence, opens the way to market leadership.

### Conclusion

Today you have again received important information about new technologies that enable you now slowly to bring together the first puzzle pieces on digitization, digitalization and digital transformation.

These examples show how important it is for you, as a board member or business owner, to be deeply involved with these topics. Because only those who understand the connections between digitization, digitalization and digital transformation today and who are able to transfer the findings to their business are among the winners of the future.

# THREE NEW YEAR'S RESOLUTIONS

*Every Automotive Dealership Should Make in 2019*

## By Sam Komeha (USA)

The New Year is a time for reflection and resolutions. It's a time when we can look back on the past year and decide what we did well and what needs to be improved. While these resolutions can be important for individuals, they can make an even bigger impact on automotive dealerships.

When businesses like automotive dealerships make resolutions, they are creating new goals for their company to achieve throughout the year. This can help keep dealerships from growing complacent and having the business stagnate. Setting a New Year's resolution at the beginning of 2019 can be just what a dealership needs to increase their business and create a brighter future.

The resolution that a dealership decides on will depend on their individual goals. However, there are three resolutions that are the most popular for companies to make. These resolutions aim to build the company, support employees, and help lead the business to success. By choosing one of these popular resolutions or deciding on a different one that fits the dealership, 2019 can be a year of untold success.

### 1. Increase Organization within the Organization

When it comes to automotive dealerships, it's impossible to be too organized. Being organized can help to eliminate stress, identify strains on profits, and make daily operations run smoothly. While most managers and owners will say that their dealership is already organized, there are usually a few portions of the business that would benefit from better planning and order.

To begin, it's important not to look at the dealership as a whole. Rather, each individual part of the dealership must be investigated separately. Throughout the year, each **section of the business**, such as sales, billing, marketing, reception, service, and any other department, **should be the focus** for a **specified amount of time**. At this time, **filing systems** can be fine-tuned, old, **unneeded documents** can be destroyed, and an easy-to-understand **organizational system can be implemented**.

As soon as the dealership is organized, operations will run much better, frustration levels will be decreased, and the whole dealership will be more cohesive.

### 2. Get Fit

When individuals make resolutions to get fit, they intend to exercise and eat better throughout the year. But, for automotive dealerships, getting fit takes on a whole new meaning. Getting a company fit can include many things, but, in general, it means **looking at weaknesses** in the dealership and trying to **eliminate** them.

Common weaknesses in a dealership include issues with employees, overspending, and customer base. When considering employees, it's important to **make sure all employees are a good fit for the company**, are happy with their work, and have the **proper resources to perform their job**. For overspending, the main issues are unnecessarily high overhead costs, paying too much for products and supplies, and not getting the most possible profit out of car sales and services. Lastly, when it comes to the customer base, dealerships may not be reaching all the potential customers in the area or may be losing customers if they aren't focusing on marketing and customer retention.

Though most dealerships won't be struggling in all these areas, it is likely that they struggle in at least one. By making the resolution to get fit for 2019, dealerships will be able to **identify what they need to work on** and continue to grow their business not just for the year, but for every year that follows.

### 3. Open Up Communication

One of the biggest complaints among employees is the lack of communication between employees and managers. When employees feel as though they can't talk to the ones who are making important company decisions, they feel helpless and under-appreciated. Dealerships wishing to retain their best employees and create an enjoyable work environment should make opening lines of communication one of their biggest goals in 2019.

To create more open lines of communication, managers and owners will have to decide what works best for their dealership. There are many ways to increase the flow of communication, including weekly meetings, having **managers visit each department** in the dealership regularly, making **time for team building** exercises, or just having certain hours each week when managers' doors are open for any employees that want to talk.

By making a small change in how employees, managers, and owners communicate, tons of wonderful things will happen for the dealership. Some great benefits include an increase in employee morale, higher customer satisfaction, and less confusion and frustration throughout the day. **Increasing communication will have the biggest impact** on a dealership of any other change they could make.

### Resolve to Make 2019 the Best Year Yet

Automotive dealership owners, managers, and employees can use the new year to motivate themselves to make long overdue changes to their business. When dealerships commit to making these changes, they can ensure their success throughout 2019 and beyond. By increasing the organization within the organization, getting fit, improving communication, or sticking to any other resolution that fits the dealership, dealerships will gain a leg up on their competition and continue to prosper for years to come.

# DECIPHERING YOUR INVESTMENT RETURNS

*Income vs. Capital Growth*

**By Kirstie Shapiro (United Kingdom)**

What is an Investment return? Simply put, **returns** are the profit that you earn from your investments.

In last month's article titled "How to integrate property into your investment portfolio for the New Year", I suggested that we could look more closely into deciphering which investment returns would suit your lifestyle best: Income Based Investment Returns or Capital Growth Investment Returns. The terminology often used for these, regarding Investment structures are 'income focused' and 'growth focused'. Do note that some investments can give you both income and growth focussed returns, however it is important to distinguish between the two, for a sound understanding and better investment acumen.

Income focused funds will deliver an investor monthly earnings, while a growth fund is focused on increasing the original sum invested as much as possible, or by a set amount, within a certain time frame. As with many investment types, property investment can generate either or both income focused and growth focused outcomes, depending on where and how you invest your money.

### INCOME Focused

This type of property investment is bought with the foremost intention of earning an income stream from it. It can be a very lucrative way to invest, when managed well. The area of focus with this type of investment is to pay attention to the **yield** that it offers which is the regular financial return to be expected.

As a stand-alone landlord, **Rental yield** can be best described as, what your tenant/s pay in rent, minus any maintenance, running costs, repairs, agents' fees, taxes etc. This yield in no way affects the original investment sum, however, it does indeed reward your investment efforts.

As a shareholder, **Dividend yield** is best described as the distribution of reward from a portion of your property investment's earnings, paid to the shareholders as per agreement, which is calculated as: Dividend Yield = Annual Dividend / Share Percentage. Whether you are a landlord or a shareholder, you will want to look at your annual return as a percentage, as this will allow you to make better comparisons with other investment products like savings accounts, ISAs, tracker funds which will give you either guaranteed Annual Equivalent Rates (AER) or non-guaranteed or 'indicative' dividends.

### GROWTH Focused

This type of investment strategy is focused on the growth of the invested capital. This type of investing can only be done with companies whose earnings are expected to grow above the average rate either of the particular industry it is in or compared with the overall market.

Property in the UK, on average, has been on the increase since 2000. Residential property has seen an average growth of 6.6% per annum and commercial property 3.7%, both of which have out-performed inflation rates of 2.8% (Retail Price Index) over the same period. As is very common with property investment, the market can fluctuate significantly and often does, with what the industry calls 'booms' (2001-2004 residential) when property prices rise and 'crashes' (2007-2008 commercial) when the property prices decline.

It must be noted that no matter which strategy you choose to be right for you, costs are incurred and taxes liable.

### Happy Investing

When deciding on what investment strategy or plan works best for you, always review your personal needs and goals. Take some time to think about what you really need and want from your investments. Not only do you need to know yourself, your needs and goals but your appetite for risk as well.

Think about how soon you will need your money back in real terms. This will affect your investment time-lines and investment types.

Make an investment plan, that helps you to diversify. Start with low risk and build up your investment muscles from there. As it is said, to enjoy a better return you need to accept more risk. A diverse investment portfolio will stand you in good stead over the longer term and helps to manage and improve the balance between risk and return.

PR MEDIA REACH　　　　　　　　THE GLOBAL PR HUB

# PR MEDIA REACH

## Get your Press Release seen by the Media

Get your newsworthy and quality business content infront of journalists around the world who need your content to make their readers and listeners happy. PRMediaReach.com offers you access to a PR Hub that connects entrepreneurs with journalist working for newspapers, magazines, radio and television broadcasters.

# 10 STEPS TO A LEAN BUSINESS & INCREASED PRODUCTIVITY

### By Robb Evans (Australia)

The *Australian Institute of Health and Welfare* reports that nearly two-thirds of adults are overweight or obese, with rates continuing to rise daily. (1) Overweight and obesity is a major public health issue in Australia and around the world and greatly contributes to risk factors of heart disease, type 2 diabetes, cancer and mental health issues. *Time* Magazine reports that obesity now costs the world $2 Trillion per year. (2) *Gallup, Duke University Medical Center* in USA report that work-related injuries of obese employees are 25% higher, medical claims costs are seven times higher and they average 10 times more days off for a work injury or illness compared to those with a healthy weight. *BMJ Open* report that of the 50 studies (3) they analysed, it was clear that there are substantial costs due to lost productivity amongst workers with obesity.

**What is obesity costing YOU and your business?**

All successful businesses have a business plan with a focus primarily on financial analysis. However, should we be measuring success with other factors in mind as well? Perhaps it's time to reflect on the operations of your own business and create a series of health metrics relating to sick leave, loss of productivity, presenteeism, turnover, death and the link between these results and the level of overweight and obese people in your business…. including yourself! What gets measured gets done! Tracking this data will enable you to draw conclusions as to the extent that the health of your employees is having on the financial performance of your business.

You wouldn't allow a recurring unnecessary cost in your business to keep draining resources if you had a solution. Right? Chances are, obesity is having a direct negative impact on your bottom line as you read this article.

Overweight and obesity issues are caused by several different factors, but by far the most common is lifestyle choices. Consuming too many calories in food and drink compared to the number of calories you are burning off through physical activity each day. As success drives your business further forward, your time can appear to be "stolen" from you, and your employees, and more excuses can be made to justify sedentary behaviours.

> **"The key is to make health a component of your business success strategy. If you or your employees aren't healthy, your business won't be as healthy, productive and profitable."- Robb Evans**

The great news is that changing sedentary behaviours to active is just a slight shift in focus each day and one of the easiest ways to reduce obesity and its risks.

There are 10 Steps you can start performing today to be more active, burn more calories and take no extra time. All that is necessary is directed attention during your work day, through simple physical activities performed consistently.

### Step #1

Park the car further away and take the stairs instead of the elevator. You can adopt this same approach when completing day-to-day tasks such as shopping, going to an appointment, running errands, etc. Every additional step made during the day adds up to more burnt calories.

### Step #2

Walk or ride your bike to work. If you take the bus or catch a train, get off a stop or two before you need and walk the rest of the way.

### Step #3

Inter-office email, messaging and the phone can be impersonal and make you lazy. Consider substituting the technology by hand delivering messages or meeting face to face to discuss an issue.

### Step #4

Look for opportunities to stand whenever you can. You burn more calories standing up than you do sitting down. Try using a standing desk or improvise with a high table or counter. Eat lunch standing up or while taking a walk.

### Step #5

Instead of taking a coffee break sitting down, go for a brisk walk. You may be surprised at how quickly the concept of walking coffee breaks amongst your friends and colleagues will catch on.

### Step #6

Get a head set for your office phone so you can walk and talk or at least move around your desk while you're still working and talking.

### Step #7

Conduct a meeting on the go. This is not something that can work all the time, but when it's practical, schedule walking or even running meetings or brainstorming sessions.

### Step #8

Consider replacing your chair with a fit ball to promote good posture. Even sitting **up straight on a chair whilst working can help you** passively work out your abdominal muscles whilst burning extra calories in the process!

### Step #9

A 10-minute workout can make a difference to the calories you burn and your overall health and well-being.

### Step #10

Embrace wearable technology to monitor your number of daily steps you take and make a conscious effort to move more during the day. Simply wearing the device and regularly referring to it creates focus and progression in your activity level. You should aim to take 10,000+ steps every day.

There are NO excuses! Implementing these 10 Steps will not only impact your own health, but will provide more productive employees, reduced absenteeism and presenteeism, decreased staff turnover and more profitability. Don't hesitate. Act now!

# 5 MOST EXPENSIVE CITIES IN AUSTRALASIA

## By John Stokoe (United Kingdom)

As **Business Booster Today** magazine has a Global reach and our readers often have a choice where they work and live, it makes sense that we look at which Cities have the most valuable real estate in the world.

Where you live makes a difference to the price you pay for property and this is often due to the demand for properties and other factors such as schools, work opportunities, leisure activities, transportation links and crime rates.

Some cities that are more expensive to live in than others and in general, properties in cities are more expensive per square meter than those in rural areas. There are different **ways of calculating** how **expensive the property** may be so to simplify it on a global scale I have used the price of property per square meter.

### 1. Hong Kong

Prices for property in Hong Kong Island are estimated at $25,551 per square meter. This is **due to limited space, low supply and high demand** and the buoyant tax friendly economy.

Another way in which value is calculated on an international scale is as used by the annual Demographia International Housing Affordability report which uses the "median multiple" ratio system, which divides median house price by gross annual median household income. Hong Kong clocked a median multiple of 18.1 which on that scale made it relatively the most expensive per population for the last 7 years.

### 2. Mumbai

While the overall real estate market in India is slowing down, this is not the case in Mumbai where property prices are soaring. One of the reasons for the property prices is that it is surrounded by water on three sides.

This makes it appealing to prospective residents, but also means that opportunities for development are limited putting properties in high demand which has resulted that in this city you can expect to pay $15,525 per square meter for a property. Mumbai is the **financial capital of India** with a population of 12 million. Other factors that drive demand are that it is home Bollywood and financial organizations like the Reserve Bank of India, the Bombay Stock Exchange, the National Stock Exchange of India, the SEBI and the corporate headquarters of different Indian and multinational organizations.

### 3. Singapore

Even though the average price per square meter of property in Singapore is $13,748 the population is continuing to rise and developers are struggling to meet the increased demand for properties. This has the significant knock on effect of positively impacting the price of properties that are available. If you want to live in Singapore, then you can expect to pay the price for doing so.

This **beautiful country attracts millions of people** from all around the world and everybody wants to live there. Singapore is **world famous due to its commerce, finance and transport hub it has strong economy** (considered 3rd highest GDP per capita) Singapore provides luxury and high standard of life with lot of facilities, such as education, healthcare, life expectancy, personal safety, and housing

### 4. Sydney

Living in an amazing city like Sydney does, however, come at a price; $7,250 per square meter to be exact. Not only Australian nationals, but also with people emigrating to Australia come because it has a **wonderful climate, fantastic work opportunities, colourful culture**.

Another reason given by experts for the high prices in Sydney are the urban containment policies. These are the government's way of preventing cities from sprawling. Instead, they encourage developments of greater density within the city. This leads to both higher land prices and higher house prices. A note is that the UBS Global Real Estate Bubble Index rates Sydney as having the world's fourth worst housing bubble risk (tied with Vancouver). So, buyers beware.

### 5. Auckland

Auckland is considered a 'global' city, so it is where many people head to establish their career forcing the price per square meter for a property in this city to around $7,082. It is a desirable place to live because of the diversity, the culture, and the vibrant atmosphere and although this has contributed to the surge in house prices, it is not the only factor.

A further cause of property inflation is the **increase in immigration to the island**, with many immigrants choosing to live in New Zealand's capital. This has led to a significant increase in the demand for property.

There are very few cities across the globe where the average house price exceeds $1 million, but that is the case and is more than double the average house price in 2007.

# BUSINESS BOOSTER TODAY
## A magazine for Entrepreneurs by Entrepreneurs

**By Louis Kotze**

A new magazine for entrepreneurs is making business people from all over the world sit up and take notice. It is called *Business Booster Today* and is the brainchild of entrepreneurial visionaries Sue Baumgaertner-Bartsch and Christian Bartsch of Munich, Germany.

I had the privilege of finding out what makes this wonderful and ever-growing magazine so popular among entrepreneurs and business people around the globe.

### 1. Sue and Christian, how and why did *Business Booster Today* begin?

*Business Booster Today* started out with a big vision, namely, to empower 20 million people around the world to grow and explode their business. As business owners, we understand the challenges of growing your business, but at the same time, we see the opportunities that come with it.

We see and meet entrepreneurs from all around the world all the time, and there are so many great ideas that people have. However, an idea is simply an idea and will not matter if you do not implement that idea and make an impact for others.

We help entrepreneurs bring that idea, service or product to fruition or help you grow to greater heights and visibility.

### 2. Where does the name "Business Booster Today" come from, and what does it say about the magazine?

Business boosters are people who take action to grow to greater heights, profits and credibility. They are people who are game changers and want to make an impact. They do not sit around and dream about ideas, but rather work at full speed to bring those ideas to fruition, and to implement the ideas with the right strategy and the right people as fast as possible. And this is exactly what we are all about.

### 3. Tell us a little more about yourselves and your love for entrepreneurship.

We both have lived and worked together on five continents and have a true passion for connecting and working with people and entrepreneurs from all around the world. The world has truly become our home.

**Sue:** When I have worked as an auditor and consultant in the US, Asia and Europe, I loved meeting with the CEOs and decision makers to learn about their business strategies and growth, but also their challenges. Working, for example, with one of the largest casinos in Asia, I had the opportunity to look behind the scenes and help them improve their strategy and controls related to their vending machine sales.

I left the corporate world after 13 years in senior management roles and transitioned into the role of an entrepreneur. Why? I believe in the freedom of making choices and realizing my own vision, as opposed to someone else's. I believe that everyone has his or her talents and gifts that were given to them in this life. It is up to us to put those into action and live to our peak potential.

I see so much potential out there in people to make a difference, but not everyone is realizing their gifts enough, because people are afraid to leave their **alleged safety** net as an employee, or they do not want to invest (enough) in themselves and their business. As n entrepreneur, international speaker and co-founder of *Business Booster Today*, I get up every morning, excited to make an impact and to help others become the best versions of themselves: to help entrepreneurs gain credibility and visibility through our magazine, and to coach them along the way in their entrepreneurial journey.

**Christian:** I was born into a multi-national family with different cultural views, beliefs and values. This makes me a very unique thinking person. I am attracted to people who treasure the benefits of travelling the world and experiencing the **variety of cultures** on this planet. I lived on several continents uniting nations that once were vicious enemies. History is one of my passions, as living and travelling gets me in contact with people and moments that influence the way we think and interact with each other. Born in Barcelona as the child of a British/German couple, it taught me to see the world from a different perspective.

I also learned that as an entrepreneur, you will experience both success and failure, but that following your passion requires you to stay persistent. This includes following through with leads that are difficult to close or not giving up on an opportunity, for example in my case, to become part of a popular science program. Once I got a government request for information on our forensic capabilities. Even though I did not have much of an expectation, I **did whatever was necessary** to provide an authentic, true and realistic report.

A few months later, to my surprise, this opened multiple doors, including speaking in front of entrepreneurs on behalf of the **security authorities** and providing knowledge to the top forensic experts of four nations behind closed doors of the **central police HQ (BKA)**. I was even recommended to speak in front of students on deep forensic technology at a special event of a German university.

When I look at entrepreneurship, I see a world with a small group of people who are following their passion to make this a better world by conducting business and working towards creating a positive legacy that will live beyond our given time on earth.

With *Business Booster Today*, Sue and I are working together as husband and wife, as mother and father, and as entrepreneurs to bring both of our talents and gifts to the world. People are now calling us "**the power couple**", and yes, together, we have the power and the passion to fuel and to reach thousands of thousands of entrepreneurs around the world to help them grow their business.

Our mission as a power couple is to build bridges between entrepreneurs, investors, philanthropists and influential people. We are connecting success on a global scale.

### 4. What makes Business Booster Today different from its competitors?

*Business Booster Today* is a magazine written by entrepreneurs for entrepreneurs. We have true entrepreneurs who are experts in their niche areas, who write, for example, about the various topics in their respective areas. This is completely different to any other business magazine where you have journalists who research a business topic and then write about it.

**Sue:** Another factor is that we are a true magazine; not just an online magazine. We have an online and a print edition. The online magazine you can be subscribed to and even download to your desktop, iPad and mobile phone.

However, anybody these days can create an online magazine and put a picture on the cover and say: "I have been on the cover of XYZ magazine", right? That is why we also have a true print magazine that gets published and that can be purchased worldwide through our website or via other retail platforms. We now have readers in 143 countries and we are still growing.

**Christian:** Another way we differentiate ourselves from the competition is that we are not only a magazine that offers various opportunities to get featured in, or to write for the magazine to become branded and visible. We also coach our clients along the way to grow in this process. For example, we coach them on how to position themselves properly, what to do with their pictures, how to increase their writing skills, and what they need to do and why. Most people can copy the how, but they cannot copy the why. Even the HOW is often a lack of business skills that people have and we guide them in all their marketing, branding and business skills so they can grow and explode their business.

### 5. Who features in your magazine, and what big names have appeared on the cover?

We have entrepreneurs from all around the world featured in our magazine. Not only entrepreneurs, but also coaches, speakers, authors, investors, philanthropists and influencers –all the way up to game changers!

The first print edition, for example, featured the World's #1 Wealth and Business Coach, JT Foxx, on the cover. We also had **Vikas Malkani**, the World's #1 Wisdom and Wealth Coach, on the cover.

In our magazine, you can also enjoy the power of top brands that are presented, such as **Aston Martin, Bentley, Tesla and BMW**.

### 6. What draws people to your magazine?

Our magazine is a shortcut to media credibility. Our clients and business partners who work with us believe in our vision and mission and enjoy our professionalism. They enjoy working with us, because we help them grow and truly provide that extra service. We go the extra mile to have happy customers, clients and business partners.

What started out as a business by ourselves has grown into a global success team – a global business booster family. We attract celebrities and industry leaders. Each edition is packed with valuable articles. We provide quality content and service online and in print!

### 7. You have recently been interviewed on the radio by a former broadcaster of CBS Radio about your magazine and entrepreneurship. What role has the media played in the magazine's success so far?

**Christian:** The media creates celebrities who become our heroes, influencers and role models. At the *age of 2*, I met my first celebrity, the big band master James Last. Even though I was really young, this was a very special moment. Little could I imagine that years later I would be meeting some of most sought-after celebrities in the world, like Mel Gibson, Jessica Simpson, Steve Wozniak and Dr Phil in the presence of fellow entrepreneurs from all across the globe!

However, at the same time, the media can deliver to us shocking news and project a view on society that might not always be in line with reality. It is thus important to always know your facts and keep an open mind!

Andy Warhol once stated that every person on earth has five minutes of fame. I personally got my first opportunity by being interviewed by the regional radio BR2 in 2011. Later followed several interviews on a popular science program broadcasted on national TV. They recorded special clips in our laboratory. After that followed interviews on a news TV channel and other radio interviews such as with "Deutsche Welle" (like BBC world service). I have also been interviewed in a German photographer magazine.

I was even once interviewed by a reporter who asked really uncomfortable questions. Knowing my duty to protect those out there in the field, I managed to outmaneuver the unpleasant questions. For me, the media is my friend who I respect and who needs to know to respect me. Yes, there are people who spread fake news out there just trying to use negativity to generate unethical profits at the cost of humans and nature. It is up to us to decide whether we let them get away with it, or if we stop them before they can use our assets to manipulate the public to hurt peace in this world.

**Sue:** As an international speaker, celebrity interviewer and guest, I have appeared on radio and TV talk shows in Germany, London, France, USA and Canada, in order to share my story and to empower others in their entrepreneurial journey.

I have shared the stage in Los Angeles with celebrities such as Mark Wahlberg, Steve Wozniak, Mel Gibson and Christie Brinkley, and even had the opportunity to interview American rapper, actor, TV host and real estate investor "Vanilla Ice" in front of over 2500 business enthusiasts from over 71 countries.

At the age of 6, I was a ballet dancer and it was my first time being and performing on stage. Later one, I was scared at first of SPEAKING up, and SPEAKING in front of larger groups. But I tackled my fears over time and became more confident as I lived and did business with various people from different cultures around the world. The media has become my friend, and I enjoy interviewing people as much as I enjoy being interviewed to inspire and empower others.

Being interviewed as a "power couple" by a former broadcaster of CBS Radio about our magazine and entrepreneurship has been fun, entertaining and key in reaching and growing our vision of reaching 20 million people to grow and explode their business.

### 8. What have been the highlights of your

journey with the magazine so far?

The year 2018 has been the year of speed of implementation to launch the "Business Booster Today" magazine, which has become the #1 German Magazine for the Global Entrepreneur. Boom!

We are extremely grateful and proud about the growth of our magazine into a global success team of over 15 amazing editors and ambassadors with readers in 143 countries in such a short amount of time.

**9. Why do you think is the magazine growing so rapidly?**

We could not have done this all by ourselves. Having the right coaches, advisors and people in our lives and businesses is key to success.

Our vision is what drives us, but what fuels us are stories of others, of people that we can help and contribute to make an impact in this world.

Lastly, it is also vital to understand that the market is changing constantly, the technology is growing, and change is inevitable. Those who adapt and change will continue to grow. As entrepreneurs and business boosters, we understand this, and we believe that we have the fuel to boost people's lives, profits, business and visibility to greater heights.

**10. Where to next for Business Booster Today?**

*Business Booster Today* ("BBT") also stands for "Building Bridges Together". This is what we are focusing on in 2019.

As entrepreneurs, we create, we cooperate and we collaborate. We have some exciting new endeavors planned; so stay tuned for more!

We are already moving full speed ahead creating new products, services and business opportunities. Having a great team of fellow

# OUR VISION

| 1 | TO EMPOWER |
| 2 | 20 MILLION PEOPLE |
| 3 | AROUND THE WORLD |
| 4 | TO GROW & EXPLODE THEIR BUSINESS |

## TOGETHER WE SUCCEED

BUSINESSBOOSTERTODAY.COM

entrepreneurs allows us to build a unique life-transforming business.

BBT is part of our global media company. Our vision and mission influence the way we plan, structure and ensure the results we are enabling people to achieve on a long-term basis. Therefore, we are expanding our media visibility domination on all channels as we see new technology and trends evolving. The numbers make us aware of the fact that we are already reaching people in 143 countries. They read, listen to and view the content that is coming from our global team.

The people behind the infrastructure that is providing printed, digital, visual and motivating physical products are growing too. We have hired great people to manage the digital technology. Our top brands are expecting us to keep up the great work. Even as we write these lines, we have leading brands in negotiation to get their products, services and businesses to be showcased. We have had awesome brands in our magazine.

Our events are going global to inspire people. The knowledge and wisdom our people have to share have to be delivered to people around the world. It is our duty to take our efforts beyond 10X and be visible in all the key ways we can empower 20 million people to change their life and business to take it to the next level.

# WHY HAVING EMPATHY AS A DOCTOR OR BUSINESS PERSON IS SO IMPORTANT TO OUR BUSINESS VITALITY

## By Michelle Davis (Germany)

### What is empathy?

The dictionary definition brings it right to the point that it is the „ability to understand and share the feelings of another ". I would describe it like a deep willingness to understand and focus on your patient or client (also business partner, coachee and/or life-partner) by listening carefully to what this person is telling you.

### Why is it so important to listen to what your patient or client tells you besides his physical or business symptoms?

Once an elderly professor at our university told us young pre-medical students this: "Make a good anamnesis - ask about the medical history, social history and current life situation – take the time and listen carefully what the patient is telling you because 80 % of the anamnesis is the diagnosis.

Already back then I was resonating with that because I had those experiences with doctors, before and after I became a medical doctor myself, who didn't really listen nor doing a physical examination. Just recently I experienced this -

„Oh you have a cold – take antibiotics" and I just asked: „don't you want to examine my lungs, my throat and make a test if it is really a bacterial cause?"

The answer was: „No when you have green mucus it is clearly bacterial"(ancient belief). Just when I told that doctor, I am a doctor myself this doctor started to change his attitude and finally examined me and took a sample – no bacteria – it was a virus! (**most of the time antibiotics are not needed!**).

This was not out of empathy and listening carefully it was **out of fear** because I was a doctor myself. I felt not taken seriously by that doctor who just assumed something. I told myself - already during my studies - I don't want to be an "*assembly-line*" (just fast symptom treating) doctor myself and till now I look for the root cause and look outside the box to find the optimal individual solution to better the vitality of my patients.

Even though I was accused quite often of being the slow doctor when I was working in surgery I always responded: "I am not slow, I am precise and often I prevented patients from extra harm." For example, one patient told me he had severe skin healing problems after a hip replacement and his surgeons didn't take him seriously. They told him he was a hypochondriac.

He was supposed to get a shoulder prosthesis at our clinic. When I looked at his hip area the skin was still strangely purple and I instantly had the suspicion of a metal allergy and cancelled the operation! My boss almost yelled at me and I just responded to have a look at his skin! Meanwhile I found out what kind of prothesis he had received for his hip which was with a nickel and cobalt alloy and I did a blood sample.

The patient trusted me and didn't want to be operated on that day and a few days later we had the **result of a nickel allergy** and my boss had to admit I was right and saved this patient an extra operation and unnecessary healing problems because he has received a titanium prothesis instead.

### Why am I telling you this story and how is this effecting the vitality of your communication, business and/or private life?

It is the same with your clients in business or your life partner. Through really listening to your clients or life partner you find out their pain and you are able to support, reduce or even eliminate that pain. What really helps as well, is when you are kind and ask interested questions and are focused on that person, for example by turning off your cell phone so no distraction can disturb this conversation.

As studies have shown if patients were treated like this from nurses and doctors - even if it was just a gesture of holding the hand of a patient who was afraid of his or her operation before he or she entered the operating room – that their recovery was faster than those who were not taken care of at all.

You can transport that to business clients and life partners as well, when their business is sick or they are struggling to succeed with certain things or when you're life partner is sick and you take real care of him or her.

So how will you improve your way of a vital communication and showing empathy to your patients, clients, business partners and/or family members today? ✒

# IS THERE OPPORTUNITY IN EMAIL MARKETING?

## By Gavin Sim (Singapore)

"Argh, another email…"

"Oh well, that is spam. Not going to open it."

"Selling me stuffs again? I am going to unsubscribe."

Does the above remind you of what you think when you receive a new email?

One of the above would most probably apply to you. **So if you could relate to it, your customers will do.**

According to research done by Radicati Group, the average person receives about 130 emails per day or about six emails per hour. To blow your mind more, there are an estimated 3.8 billion email users. If we do the mathematics, there are close to **23 billion emails begin sent every hour**.

**Is there an opportunity there? Definitely.**

The question is, "Do you know **how to make use of this opportunity**?"

If you don't, read on because I am going to share with you the exact thing you need to do to profit as much as possible from emails. Even if you are sending emails now, there are also a few tips and tricks that you could get from this article.

1. Building Your Email List

This would be the very first thing you have to do to profit from email marketing. In our industry, there is a saying **"List is King."** Nothing would be further from the truth. Your list is the one thing that is going to bring you profits, but how do you build a list?

It is very simple today. Compared to ten years ago when a website must be build using complicated and confusing codes that would take a novice month(s) (an expert probably days), you can build a functioning website in minutes today! Even with no experience!

That is very crucial because you would need to build a squeeze page. On that page, you would usually **offer something free to the visitors, and in exchange, obtain their name and email address.**

I would recommend getting an email auto-responder service to help you store the data that you have collected as they would come in very useful to help you mass send your emails or to set up automated campaigns.

2. Sending Emails

Cool! Now that you have built a list, it is not going to make you any money if you leave it sitting there. For starters, there are two common mistakes that I see clients and students do all the time. The errors are self-explanatory, but **they are crucial**. Let me explain more.

a. Selling too much

For the first group, they sell way too much. By that, I mean sending at least two sales emails per day. Most people do this mistake because they wanted to milk their database as much as possible. Ultimately, this is why you built the list in the first place… Right?

However, by sending too much sales emails, people associate you with spammers or someone who merely wants to earn a quick buck. That puts people off, and your database will shrink as **people unsubscribe or become unresponsive** as they stop opening your emails.

b. Not selling at all

The second group learns the lesson from the first group, and they don't send email to sell. However, they become afraid to do so and most NEVER sent any email to sell products. **No selling means no revenue.**

Your business requires sales to sustain itself. Let's face it. You still have your overheads to pay for, and money is not going to fall from the sky. It comes from selling products through your list.

The key here is to… **maintain a balance.**

Inbox Income Academy shows our clients and students to use a formula called **VVSVVT**. VVSVVT stands for Value, Value, Sales, Value, Value, Target. That is the sequence of emails that gave us the **best results in terms of engagement and sales**.

a. Value Emails

These emails should provide information that is valuable to the prospect. For example, if you are targeting people who want to lose weight, this email could be an email that shares tips and tricks to lose more weight but still being able to eat whatever they wanted.

b. Sales Emails

Following the value emails, you should send a sales email promoting a product based on the previous Value Emails. For example, if you were sending weight loss tips previously, you should send an email to sell a weight loss product.

c. Target Emails

These emails are pseudo-sales emails. What you want to do here is to provide your subscriber some kind of value which has a sales funnels at the back end. For example, you may send your subscribers a free eBook on weight loss that has tracking links which could attribute a sale to you if they buy a product.

3. Selling just… Once

This is another mistake that we see all the time.

It is essential for you to understand that **sales do not usually happen upon first contact**. Based on research by Salesforce, it takes at least six interactions before a lead is even "sales qualified". That is why the VVSVVT framework comprises of six emails.

In fact, for each campaign that you set up for a product or service, Inbox Income Academy recommends that you do **at least two cycles of VVSVVT**. That equates to a minimum of 12 emails. This should help you bring up your conversion rate.

You may ask why there are so many interactions needed.

There are many reasons, but I would typically explain this based on two principles.

a. Know, Like, and Trust

People buy from others whom they like and trust better (apart from family and friends). For your subscribers to buy from you, they need to know you better through the emails. By sending them personalised emails, they will get to know you. By providing them with valuable information, they will get to like you. Over time, you will gain their trust, and that is when you start making sales.

b. Law of Reciprocity

You would also realise that I have been talking about adding value to people. This is because the Law of Reciprocity states that when someone does something nice for you, you will develop a deep-rooted psychological urge to do something nice in return. In many cases, you may even reciprocate with a gesture far more generous than the original deed.

In our context, by providing value to your subscribers, they may feel the urge to buy something from you to return the favour.

So, with **more than 3.07 billion USD being generated in 2018**, I am sure there is an opportunity in Email Marketing. What I shared could be applied in both the corporate world as well as individual starting a small online business. I wish you all the best in achieving email marketing success.

If you ever need more information, feel free to reach out to Gavin (gavin@inboxincomeacademy.com) or visit their page (www.InboxIncomeAcademy.com) to opt in for their free 4-days Video Masterclass. You can also find Inbox Income Academy on Facebook where they put up free webinars every Tuesday.

**BUSINESS BOOSTER TODAY MAGAZINE**

PRESENTS

# START!

BUSINESS BOOSTER TODAY
Available in eJournal Section after Lufthansa Checkin

**Available for all Classes**
on all Lufthansa flights worldwide

## Opportunities?

**Advertising**

- Products
- Services
- Introduction

## Devices?

- Smartphones
- Tablets
- Notebooks

**Contact:**
info@businessboostertoday.com

# BUSINESS INTRODUCTIONS

## BIOVETA - BEAUTIFUL HAIR SHAMPOO PRODUCTS

Bioveta is a family of unique products which provide synergistic support in a very organic and sophisticated manner. We supply revolutionary products that work. Bioveta's advanced research ensures that we provide and maintain the absolute finest products available to date. From your hair to your toes, inside and out, Bioveta has a plan to create a whole new healthier you.

BioVeta, LLC, Dallas, Texas, USA

www.bioveta.com

---

## AUTOMOTIVE SERVICE TAGS REDUCE COSTS & WASTE

We have insider knowledge of dealerships and their service departments, which gives us the opportunity to look at the wasteful, ineffective areas of the industry and develop products to make them more efficient. Currently, one of the most unnecessary costs of dealership service departments is the thousands of dollars' worth of paper auto service tags they throw away each year.

New Generation Service Tags, LLC, Chevy Chase, MD, USA

www.newgenerationservicetags.com

---

## WE BOOST MEDIA CREDIBILITY AND VISIBILITY

Do you want to diversify your business into multiple countries? This seams an impossible task? It is all too complicated to get the international marketing for your brand going? We will boost your sales by 30% in 90 days with our strategies and platforms. Don't waste your energy and budget on experiments!

PR Media Reach, Munich, Germany

www.PRMediaReach.com

---

## GENERATE INCOME WITH PROPERTY IN VESTMENT IN THE UK

Learn how to successfully master the property investment in business. Our trainers are successful real estate investors with expertise in the banking and sourcing business. Our workshops provide you the knowledge so that deals come to you and how to create for yourself a bullet proof investor package. Our clients are successful in sourcing, generating returns of investment and building a recurring amount of deals with their investors.

Source My Property LTD, Cardiff, United Kingdom

www.SourceMYProperty.com/academy

---

## MUMS ARE SUCCESSFUL FAMILY AND BUSINESS LEADERS

We help mum's who work from home to create a balanced, abundant life filled with fun and laughter. We have everything you need in one place. Here at Mum Academy we nurture you to give you the power to nurture yourself. We do this through virtual business coaching, conferences, global retreats, online peer support, inspirational reading, online courses and training videos.

Mum Academy, Cardiff, United Kingdom

www.mumacademy.com

---

## ADVERTISING IN THIS SECTION

**Want to be part of this advertising section?**

**Schedule a consultation call via https://meetme.so/bbtmag or send us an email to info@businessboostertoday.com**

www.ingramcontent.com/pod-product-compliance
Lightning Source LLC
Chambersburg PA
CBHW040057250526
45473CB00043B/1850